PREACHER™
Dixie Fried

Featuring
CASSIDY: BLOOD & WHISKEY
A Tale from the Good Ol' Days

GARTH ENNIS
Writer

STEVE DILLON
Artist

MATT HOLLINGSWORTH
PAMELA RAMBO
JAMES SINCLAIR
Colorists

CLEM ROBINS
Letterer

GLENN FABRY
Original Covers

PREACHER
created by
Garth Ennis and Steve Dillon

I AM.

MY NAME IS ECCARIUS.

CASSIDY.

I MUST'VE SMELLED YEH FROM TEN MILES OUT'VE TOWN. I'VE NEVER MET ANOTHER, YEH KNOW, ANOTHER ONE BEFORE. EXCEPT WHEN I GOT BIT, OBVIOUSLY...

TO TELL YEH THE TRUTH, I SOMETIMES THOUGHT I WAS THE ONLY ONE.

THE WIND BROUGHT ME SCENT OF YOUR PASSING, TOO.

NO, MY FRIEND, YOU ARE NOT ALONE IN THE DARKNESS. YOU ARE LIKE ME, A LORD OF NIGHTFALL, PIERCING VEINS AND DRINKING CRIMSON, WALKING IN THE SHADOWS OF THE MORTAL WORLD...

THEY FEAR US, AND BANISH US TO THE BLACKNESS OF THEIR NIGHTMARES--YET THERE WE FLOURISH, AND GROW STRONG...

FOR WHAT ARE WE, BUT THE EVIL IN THEIR OWN HEARTS?

WE ARE A DARK MIRROR TO THEM, REFLECTING BACK THEIR SELF-DOUBT AND SELF-LOATHING.

WE ARE--

AW, FUCK ME...!

I'M SORRY?

YEH'RE A WANKER, AREN'T YEH?

13

"WANKER"...IS THAT ONE OF THE MORE WESTERN-EUROPEAN TRANSLATIONS?

TRANSLATION?

MM. OF WHAMPYRE.

ARE YOU TAKIN' THE FUCKIN' PISS?

IT MEANS YEH SPEND TOO MUCH TIME PLAYIN' WI' YER-SELF. YEH'VE GOT YER HEAD STUCK UP YER OWN ARSEHOLE. *WANKER: NOUN. ONE WHO WANKS.*

AM I GETTIN' THROUGH TO YEH, DO YEH THINK?

ALL RIGHT, LOOK, I'M SORRY. I KNOW THIS IS YER PLACE AN' EVERYTHING. IT'S JUST A BIT OF A...WELL, A DISAPPOINTMENT, REALLY.

HOW SO?

BECAUSE I'VE BEEN WANDERIN' ROUND THE WORLD FOR THREE QUARTERS OF A FUCKIN' CENTURY, WATCHIN' ALL ME MATES DYIN' OR GETTIN' OLD, AN' NOW I FINALLY FIND SOMEONE ELSE WHO'S GONNA LIVE FOREVER AN'--

WELL.

IT TURNS OUT HE'S A BIT'VE A PRICK.

YOU SPOKE OF LOSING LOVED ONES AND COMPANIONS, CASSIDY. IT IS *EVER* OUR BURDEN, WE WHO STAND APART FROM MORTAL MAN.

AND YET, PERHAPS, YOU WILL FIND MORE SOLACE IN THIS CITY THAT YOU MIGHT AT FIRST HAVE THOUGHT.

OH AYE?

THERE ARE OTHERS HERE WHO WOULD FORSAKE THE SUNLIT WORLD, AND SURRENDER TO OUR DARK AND SCARLET URGING...

THERE'S MORE LIKE US, YEH MEAN?

NOT EXACTLY.

A SOCIETY THAT CONGREGATES IN A CELLAR DEEP BENEATH THE QUARTER, AND WHICH I SOMETIMES VISIT. THEY COVET THE LIFE THAT WE ALONE CAN LIVE, AND SEEK TO EMULATE IT...

AH. THEY AMUSE ME.

HOW COULD THEY KNOW THE TORMENT THAT WE FACE? OF NEVER QUITE BELONGING, ALWAYS LOOKING IN FROM OUT HERE IN THE COLD...THE EXQUISITE HELL OF A LIFE BOTH BLESSED AND CURSED...

AYE. TORMENT.

AT NEXT NIGHTFALL I WILL TAKE YOU TO THEM.

BUT COME, THE SUN IS RISING. OUR TIME IS ENDED. WE MUST REST.

I HAVE A PLACE PREPARED FOR YOU.

I THOUGHT I'D LOST YOU IN THE CROWD, MY FRIEND.

AYE...LISTEN, YEH COULDN'T FUCK OFF AN' DO IT AGAIN, COULD YEH? CAUSE--

COME. WE MUST AWAY.

THIS IS NO PLACE FOR THE LIKES OF US. WE ARE EXPECTED AT A GATHERING BENEATH THE STREETS, AND THERE WE MUST HASTEN, AND GO DOWN.

er...

THERE OUR FAMILIARS AWAIT US, FAR AWAY FROM PRYING EYES. THERE WE MAY COMMIT THE DARK AND SECRET ACTS THAT OUR KIND LONG FOR, SAFE FROM HINDRANCE AND PERSECUTION.

COME, MY FRIEND! THE NIGHT AWAITS!

IT'S...IT'S NOT WHAT YEH THINK...

I LIKE HIS BATMAN OUTFIT.

THEY ARE SO LIKE CHILDREN, AREN'T THEY? SO FULL OF GAY ABANDON, NEVER SUSPECTING WHAT WAITS IN THE TWILIGHT AFTER CHILDHOOD'S END...

TO THINK THAT YOU AND I WERE ONCE LIKE THEM, *mm?*

SHOW YOUR TITS! SHOW YOUR TITS! SHOW YOUR TITS!

I STILL REMEMBER~HOW COULD I FORGET? THE NIGHT I WAS PIERCED, AND DRAINED, AND THEN REBORN.

CHRISTENED IN CRIMSON: A NATIVITY OF MOONLIGHT AND NIGHTMARE.

BEFORE, I WAS NO ONE SPECIAL. MY LIFE WAS DULL ROUTINE.

ROLLING HOME ONE NIGHT, A DRUNKEN FOOL LOST ON THE OUTSKIRTS OF TOWN, I STUMBLED ON A ROW OF SKIFFS TIED AT THE BAYOU'S EDGE--AND RESTED THERE A WHILE.

SOMETHING CAME UPON ME FROM THE WATER.

SOMETHING... *ANCIENT...*

THROUGH THE VODKA-HAZE I GLIMPSED A FLASH OF BLAZING EYES, OF GLEAMING FANGS. A GOUT OF BLOOD SHOT HIGH IN THE NIGHT, AND I WAS GONE.

THE MORNING SUN BROUGHT AGONIZING FIRE, AND I SLIPPED BENEATH THE WATER MY ASSAILANT HAD EMERGED FROM, AND NEVERMORE SAW THAT KILLING YELLOW EYE.

NO, NOR DID I MEET THE *OTHER* AGAIN, WHO SET ME FREE FROM LIFE:

AND TRAPPED ME IN THE NIGHT FOREVER.

THIS IS *CASSIDY*, CHILDREN. HE IS ONE OF US.

ONE OF US...?

NO, LILI. ONE OF *US*.

HOLY SHIT...!

COOL.

MMM. I *DO* DECLARE.

YOU CAN SEE HOW THEY FIND THEIR PLEASURES. THEY CALL THEMSELVES *LES ENFANTS DU SANG*...

OH, WELL THAT'S PRETTY FUCKIN' ORIGINAL.

THEY HAVE THEIR USES. LILI'S FATHER IS A LOCAL CONGRESSMAN.

AYE, IN OTHER WORDS THEY'RE A PACK OF PONCEY GOTHIC RICH-KID WANNABES. HAVE YOU NO FUCKIN' SHAME?

ECCARIUS? *SORRY* TO INTERRUPT...

ROGER.

HHHH.

WHAT'S THE MATTER NOW?

CAND FIND BY CONTACND LENDS.

SHIT, YEH MEAN TO SAY YER EYES AREN'T REALLY THAT COLOR?

DO YEH SMOKE?

...YES.

HAIR DYED TOO, WHA'?

MM. THOD I-- HNFF--THOUGHT I OUGHT TO TRY AND LOOK THE PART.

WHAT PART?

DNO.

YOU KNOW. A NIGHTWALKER. A LORD OF THE UNDEAD.

AAOW!

WHAT WAS THAT FOR?

FOR TALKIN' SHITE. FROM NOW ON YEH GET A CLIP ROUND THE EAR EVERY TIME YEH ACT THE PRICK, RIGHT?

YEH'VE BEEN GOIN' ABOUT THIS COMPLETELY THE WRONG WAY. YEH NEED SORTIN' OUT, SON.

AN' I'M JUST THE BOY TO DO THE SORTIN'.

I'M SUDDENLY NOT REALLY IN MUCH OF A PARTY MOOD. ISN'T THERE ANYWHERE QUIETER ROUND HERE?

WE COULD GO BACK TO MY HOME.

FUCKIN' MILES AWAY. CAN'T BE ARSED.

AH!

MM?

ARE YOU INSANE?!

WHY NOT? ALL THE PEACE AN' QUIET YEH COULD WANT.

IT'S HOLY GROUND! IT'S SACRED!

IT'LL KILL US STONE AAOW!

DON'T SAY I DIDN'T WARN YEH. WHAT'RE YEH SO BLEEDIN' SCARED OF?

THE CROSS, FOR ONE THING.

AAOW!

DON'T BE A FUCKIN' EEJIT! WHAT'RE YEH SCARED'VE CROSSES FOR, 'CAUSE SOME BOLLICKS GOT NAILED TO ONE A COUPLE'VE THOUSAND YEARS AGO?

BUT--

GET IN THERE!

BE GOOD BLEEDIN' THERAPY FOR YEH...

SO WHY'RE YEH AFRAID'VE THAT THING?

WELL...I REALLY DON'T WANT TO GET HIT AGAIN, BUT I SORT OF THOUGHT IT WENT WITH THE TERRITORY...

WHY?

BECAUSE--YOU KNOW. BECAUSE IT ALWAYS DOES.

ALWAYS MEANIN' IN NOVELS AN' MOVIES AN' SPOOKY OUL' STORIES, AYE?

JUST AS A MATTER'VE INTEREST, WHAT'D YEH DO, ONCE YEH TWIGGED ON WHAT'D HAPPENED TO YEH?

I...WELL, WHEN I STARTED BURNING UP IN THE SUN AND GETTING THE BLOODLUST, I KNEW THERE WAS REALLY ONLY ONE THING IT COULD BE. I MEAN EVERYONE'S SEEN *DRACULA* AT LEAST ONCE...

SO I SORT OF READ UP ON IT. OBVIOUSLY THERE'S NO ACTUAL TEXTBOOK ON THE BEHAVIOR OF OUR KIND, SO--

SO YEH WENT BY WHAT ALL THE TOSSY FUCKIN' NOVELS SAID.

UM...YES. THE LIFESTYLE SORT'VE APPEALED TO ME, I SUPPOSE.

YOU KNOW.

THE GOTHIC THING.

SUPPOSE YEH'RE AN ORDINARY FELLA, NOT LIKE US, AN' YEH'RE IN A PLANE CRASH IN THE FUCKIN' JUNGLE. NO OTHER SURVIVORS. NO SIGNS'VE CIVILIZATION. YEH'RE STRANDED.

BY SOME MIRACLE, YEH STUMBLE ACROSS A COPY OF TARZAN OF THE APES. YEH READ IT.

DO YEH GO AN' LIVE IN THE TREETOPS AN' TALK TO MONKEYS?

POINT.

DON'T GET ME WRONG, I FUCKIN' LOVE DRACULA. READ IT LOADS'VE TIMES. BUT EVERY TIME I GET TO THE END I THINK-- WHAT AN ARSEHOLE!

NO FUCKIN' WAY ARE THEY GONNA GET ME LIKE THAT!

AH, JAYSIS.

YEH KNOW...WHEN I THINK OF THE STUFF I'VE GOT UP TO IN ME TIME--AN' YEH SHOULD FUCKIN' SEE SOME'VE IT, I'M TELLIN' YEH-- IT JUST MAKES ME THINK HOW LUCKY WE ARE BEIN' LIKE THIS, YEH KNOW?

WE'VE THE WHOLE WIDE WORLD OUT THERE WAITIN' FOR US, AN' WE'VE FOREVER TO MAKE THE MOST'VE IT. AN' THAT'S THE THING, MATE: ENJOYIN' LIFE.

NOT LIVIN' DEATH, OR ANY- THIN' STUPID LIKE THAT.

AN' SURE WHAT'VE WE GOT TO FEAR EXCEPT THE SUN?

CHRIST, WHAT A SAD COLLECTION OF LOSERS, MM?

TOO MUCH TIME ON THEIR HANDS, MATE. LEADS TO POETRY.

I'M SURPRISED I DIDN'T JUST DRAIN THE LOT OF THEM YEARS AGO.

AYE, BUT THEY'RE NOT ACTUALLY WORTH KILLIN', ARE THEY?

OH, NO.

NAH, YEH WOULDN'T WANNA DO A THING LIKE THAT.

...HAVE YEH KILLED?

YOU ASKED ME ABOUT THAT BEFORE. I...WELL.

I'M NOT SAYING IT HASN'T HAPPENED.

BUT IT'S NOT A REGULAR THING.

NO.

NAH, BLOOD'S BLOOD, ISN'T IT? DOESN'T MATTER IF YEH GET IT FROM A LAMB CHOP, SO LONG AS YEH GET YER FILL.

NO NE__ FOR KILLIN' AT ALL, REALLY.

UNLESS SOME PRICK TRIES TO DO FOR YOU, IN WHICH CASE YEH MAY AS WELL GO AHEAD AN' TREAT YERSELF.

SHE CALLED ME. I COULDN'T RESIST.

IT'S WHAT SHE WANTED, YOU SEE.

IT'S WHAT THEY ALWAYS WANT.

THEY BEG AND BEG AND BEG...AND THEY'RE SO SURE THEY'LL LOVE THIS LIFE, MYSTERIOUS AND BEAUTIFUL AND *DARK*...

EXCEPT I ALWAYS TAKE *TOO MUCH*.

YEH HAD TO GO.

YEH WERE TOO MUCH OF A WANKER TO LIVE.

AN' YEH MAYBE BROUGHT BACK TOO MANY BAD MEMORIES.

AN' YEH WERE RIGHT ABOUT TRYNNA CHANGE PEOPLE.

THEY LIKE THEIR OUL' SHITE TOO MUCH.

FIRST SIGN OF MADNESS...

HOW'RE YEH! I DIDN'T THINK YEH WERE WORKIN' TONIGHT. DIDN'T SEE YEH.

JUST PICKING UP MY PAYCHECK. SO WHAT IS IT BRINGS YOU HERE, STARING MEANINGFULLY INTO YOUR BEER AND MUTTERING TO YOURSELF?

N.Y.C.:

WELL, BEEN NICE KNOWIN' YOU...

GET ON IN THERE AN' STOP BEIN' SUCH A BIG DRAMA QUEEN. SHE'S BOUND TO'VE CALMED DOWN BY NOW.

SURE, ALL I DID WAS STRAND HER IN THE MIDDLE OF GODDAMN FRANCE. SHE'S PROBABLY FORGOTTEN ALL ABOUT IT.

I'M SURE SHE'LL LET YEH OFF WI' JUST A LIGHT MAIMIN'...

AHA HA HA. GUESS I'LL BE SEEIN' YOU.

OR NOT.

BABY!

MMMMMWAHH!

WHERE THE HELL IS THAT FUCKWIT HOOVER?

HE DISAPPEARED COMPLETELY, HERR STARR. I CAN ONLY ASSUME THAT CUSTER KILLED HIM.

MM.

SO?

WHAT D'YOU MEAN, SO?

SO, ARE YOU GOING TO TELL ME WHAT HAPPENED IN MASADA?

OH, WELL LET ME SEE: WE HAD AN ANGEL, A WHORE, A EUNUCH, SEVERAL DOZEN IDIOTS, AN UNKILLABLE MICK, A ONE-MAN HOLOCAUST IN A DUSTER COAT, THE OCCASIONAL TWENTY-COURSE BANQUET FOR THE MOTHER OF ALL FAT FUCKERS, INBREEDING, FAMILY FEUDS, BULIMIA, A RETARDED CHILD--ALWAYS GOOD FOR A LAUGH--

AND THE UTTER DESTRUCTION OF OUR MOST SACRED SHRINE AND SECRET RETREAT IN THE DETONATION OF A FIFTY-TON BOMB.

AND WE ALSO HAD JESSE CUSTER...

ANYWAY, IF I REMEMBER ANY MORE, I'LL BE SURE TO LET YOU KNOW.

THERE'S NO NEED TO BE SARCASTIC.

ACTUALLY, FEATHERSTONE, THERE IS EVERY NEED TO BE SARCASTIC.

AND WHAT ARE WE DOING IN THIS WRETCHED LITTLE SHITHOLE? DON'T TELL ME THE BUDGET'S FUCKED AS WELL...

NOT AT ALL. I SIMPLY FELT THAT AFTER THE GUNFIGHT AT THE DeSADE MANSION, IT MIGHT BE BEST TO MAINTAIN A LOW PROFILE FOR A WHILE.

HORSESHIT, I WANT THE RITZ. AND IF ANYONE COMPLAINS ABOUT OUR PROFILE I'LL PHONE BILL CLINTON AND HAVE THE FUCKERS SHIPPED TO SOME GULAG IN ALASKA.

YOU CAN DO THAT KIND OF THING WHEN YOU'RE ALL-FATHER OF THE GRAIL.

OH, I'M EXAGGERATING. BUT IT'S LIKE THIS IS EVEN WORSE THAN THE LAST TIME, YOU KNOW, WHEN HE LEFT ME IN PHOENIX? HE HAD AN EXCUSE FOR THAT. BUT THIS...

YEAH?

WE WERE IN SOME TROUBLE, OKAY? SO HE MADE SURE I WAS NICE AND SAFE AND THEN HE SNEAKED OFF AND TOOK CARE OF BUSINESS HIMSELF. HE COULDN'T EVEN TRUST ME TO WATCH MY OWN ASS, I FELT LIKE SUCH A HANDICAP...

WELL...THAT SUCKS AND EVERYTHING, AND HE'S DEFINITELY AN ASSHOLE FOR DOING IT, BUT IF THIS IS THE SAME JESSE CUSTER WE'RE TALKING ABOUT I CAN'T BELIEVE YOU'RE SURPRISED...

I KNOW...

AND IT'S NOT LIKE HE DID IT TO SPITE YOU...

I KNOW...

I KNOW, I KNOW, I KNOW. LOOK, I'M HAVING A HARD ENOUGH TIME STAYING PISSED AT HIM WITHOUT YOU PLEADING HIS CASE, BELIEVE ME. I REALLY JUST FEEL HURT MORE THAN ANYTHING ELSE.

YOU'RE RIGHT, YOU KNOW THAT? WE WERE MEANT FOR EACH OTHER. YOU DON'T GET GUYS LIKE HIM ANYMORE, ALL BIG AND TOUGH AND GOOD AND KIND, ALL AT THE SAME TIME...

IF YOU DO, I CERTAINLY NEVER MET THEM.

EXCEPT FOR YOUR DAD?

EXCEPT FOR MY DAD.

HONEY, LISTEN TO ME. I WOULD PAY MONEY FOR A CHANCE TO JUMP YOUR BOYFRIEND'S BONES, AND I'M TELLING YOU: GIVE HIM ANOTHER CHANCE.

PLEASE.

SEE IF YOU CAN PUT ME IN A GOOD MOOD, THEN. TELL ME ABOUT YOUR LOVE LIFE.

JUST BROKE UP.

OOP!

NO, NO, IT'S FINE. BELIEVE ME.

SPILL THE BEANS, GIRL!

OKAY, SO I'M GOING OUT WITH THIS GUY NIGEL. HE WRITES, YOU KNOW? JUST SHORT FICTION, NOTHING MAJOR YET...

SO HE SEEMS PRETTY NICE, AND WE'VE BEEN DATING A FEW WEEKS, AND WE'RE GETTING COMFORTABLE-- WE'RE NOT READY TO MOVE IN OR ANYTHING, BUT WE TRUST EACH OTHER ENOUGH TO BE INTIMATE, YEAH?

GOOD TOGETHER, BUT NOT A CUTE COUPLE.

EXACTLY. SO WE'LL BE ALONE, TALKING, AND HE'S ASKING ME ALL THESE QUESTIONS: STUFF ABOUT WHAT'S IT LIKE FOR GIRLS WHEN YOU'RE GROWING UP, LIKE WHEN YOUR BOOBS START TO GROW, AND TIME OF THE MONTH, AND LOSING IT AND SO ON-- WHAT IT FEELS LIKE FOR US, BASICALLY.

I ASK HIM WHY HE WANTS TO KNOW, AND HE SAYS HE'S ALWAYS WONDERED, AND LIKE I SAY WE'RE AT THE PILLOW-TALK STAGE...

SO I TELL HIM.

SO HE GOES AND WRITES THIS FUCKING HORROR NOVEL, THIS TRASHY, MISOGYNIST, DERIVATIVE PIECE OF HUMORLESS SHIT CALLED *RAZORVILLE*--

AND HE PUTS *EVERY FUCKING THING* I TOLD HIM IN IT.

SO YOU KNOW WE WERE TALKING ABOUT ROY? FROM MEMPHIS?

YEAH?

OH, WELL THIS WILL TOTALLY GROSS YOU OUT-- 'SCUSE--

SHIT! ANYWAY, YOU REMEMBER HE WORE THOSE O.J.-TYPE GLOVES ALL THE TIME, THOSE TIGHT BLACK GLOVES? THOUGHT THEY MADE HIM LOOK LIKE A HITMAN OR SOMETHING?

I FINALLY FOUND OUT WHY HE WORE THEM.

HAIRY PALMS?

SAUSAGE... FINGERS...

SAUSAGE FINGERS! COMING TO GET YOU, O'HARE! ALL FAT AND SHORT AND STUBBY AND SWEATY AND EEEUUGGHH!

AAH! NO! GROSS!

BEYOND GROSS! COULDN'T EVEN FIT 'EM IN THE TRIGGER GUARD!

OH, STOP IT!

IMAGINE THEM TOUCHING YOU--!

RUMORS OF WAR

GARTH ENNIS - Writer   STEVE DILLON - Artist

MATT HOLLINGSWORTH - Colorist

CLEM ROBINS - Letterer   AXEL ALONSO - Editor

PREACHER created by GARTH ENNIS and STEVE DILLON

YOU KNOW WHAT THE WORST THING ABOUT IT WAS...?

WHAT WAS THE WORST THING, BABY?

IT REMINDED ME OF WHEN I WAS EIGHT AND THE BOYS WOULDN'T LET ME PLAY SOLDIERS.

I MEAN, I HAD MORE ISSUES OF SERGEANT ROCK THAN ANY OF THEM, AND I KNEW ALL THE LINES IN *BATTLE OF THE BULGE* OFF BY HEART--BUT OH NO. YOU CAN'T PLAY. YOU'RE A *GIRL*.

AND WHEN YOU DUMPED ME IN THAT MOTEL AND RAN OFF ON YOUR BIG BOY'S ADVENTURE, I FELT JUST AS DUMB AND USELESS AND STUPID AS THEY MADE ME FEEL ALL THOSE YEARS AGO.

WELL...UH... I AIN'T TRYNNA GET OFF THE SUBJECT HERE OR ANYTHING, HONEY, BUT I REALLY GOTTA ASK...

HOW COME YOU WANTED TO PLAY SOLDIERS, INSTEADA LIKE WITH DOLLS AN' STUFFED TOYS AN' SHIT LIKE THAT?

REMIND ME WHY I HAVE SEX WITH YOU AGAIN?

BABY?

MM?

WHAT WERE YOU SO UPSET ABOUT WHEN YOU GOT BACK THIS MORNIN'?

... IT WAS JUST, YOU KNOW, I GUESS I THOUGHT ENOUGH WAS ENOUGH. LIKE CUFFING YOU TO THE BED AND LEAVING YOU WAS A GREAT IDEA, BUT ACTUALLY GOING THROUGH WITH IT GOT HARDER AND HARDER TO DO...

WE'LL SEE. SO WHAT HAVE YOU BEEN UP TO SINCE YOU GOT INTO TOWN?

HANGIN' OUT WITH CASS, MOSTLY.

I TELL YOU, SEEIN' HIM KINDA GROWIN' BACK TOGETHER, THAT WAS SOME CRAZY SHIT, AN' HE TOLD ME HIS LIFE STORY, WHICH WAS SORTA LIKE IF BRENDAN BEHAN FUCKED BRAM STOKER AN' THEY LET THE BABY DO CRACK ALL THE TIME...

HE DID A REAL NICE THING, TOO. YOU KNOW WHAT HE SAID TO ME?

WHAT?

NO SHIT. NEXT TIME, DON'T WAIT SIX OR SEVEN HOURS BEFORE GIVIN' IN TO YOUR CONSCIENCE, OKAY?

SAID HE WAS GONNA STICK BY ME.

HE'S GONNA STAY AROUND UNTIL THIS THING GETS DONE.

PLAN B.

HEY...

HEY, ANNIE OAKLEY. NICE PLACE YOU PICKED.

THIS IS WHERE THE *BOYS* DRINK. CAN I GET A BLOODY MARY AND ANOTHER CLUB SODA, PLEASE?

SURE.

ARE THEY JOINING US?

SPECIAL GUN!
NEW .455 MAGNUM
WHAT IT'LL DO TO YOUR MOTHERFUCKING HEAD

YEAH, BUT I'M KIND OF GLAD YOU SHOWED UP FIRST...

YEAH, YOU SAID ON THE PHONE! THIS GUY CASSIDY, WHAT THE FUCK IS THAT ALL ABOUT...?

I DON'T KNOW. I'M STILL TOTALLY FREAKED OUT BY THE WHOLE THING.

DID YOU SAY ANYTHING TO JESSE?

OH CHRIST, I COULDN'T...

IT WOULD FUCK HIM UP TOTALLY. HE TRUSTS CASSIDY, HE REALLY LIKES HIM-- IT'S "CASS THIS, CASS THAT..."

I MEAN I LIKED HIM TOO. I THOUGHT HE WAS A REAL CLOWN, BUT FUN TO HAVE AROUND, YOU KNOW? BUT JESSE THINKS THE GUY SHITS GOLD...

HONESTLY, AMY. IT'D WRECK *EVERYTHING*.

WHAT'S SO SPECIAL ABOUT HIM?

WELL, YOU KNOW HOW JESSE MAKES SUCH A BIG DEAL ABOUT HONOR AND LOYALTY? I MEAN, IT'S A VERY GUY THING TO DO...

I GUESS IT'S A GIRL THING, TOO. BUT WE DON'T HAVE TO TURN EVERYTHING INTO AN IDEAL, WE JUST GET ON WITH IT.

WE DON'T READ ENOUGH HEMINGWAY.

ANYWAY, CASSIDY SEEMS TO MEET JESSE'S STANDARDS IN THAT REGARD. HE THINKS OL' CASS IS A REAL BUDDY, A STRAIGHT SHOOTER. GUY'D GO TO HELL FOR YOU.

HE SHOULD HAVE HEARD THE SHIT THE PRICK WAS COMING OUT WITH LAST NIGHT...

GUYS JUST DON'T GET IT. YOU CAN'T *REALLY* KNOW ANYONE, UNTIL YOU SEE HOW THEY ACT TRYNNA GET INTO YOUR PANTS...

WHAT ARE YOU GONNA DO, BABE?

I DON'T HAVE THE SLIGHTEST IDEA.

AW NO--I NO, DON'T, NOW! IT'D FUCKIN' DESTROY HIM!

YEAH, I KNOW. IT WOULD ABSOLUTELY BREAK HIM IN TWO. AND THAT'S THE ONLY THING STOPPING ME FROM TELLING HIM.

HE'S DEVOTED TO YOU, YOU KNOW THAT? I'VE NEVER REALLY KNOWN HIM TO HAVE A CLOSE FRIEND BEFORE. WITH THE LIFE HE'S HAD, HE'S GOT *VERY* HIGH STANDARDS OF WHAT HE CONSIDERS A GOOD GUY--

BUT YOU *KNEW* HOW TO PUSH ALL THE RIGHT BUTTONS WITH HIM RIGHT FROM THE BEGINNING, *DIDN'T YOU?*

AW, TULIP... I MEAN...YEH'RE MAKIN' IT SOUND LIKE I PLANNED THIS, LIKE IT WAS ALL CALCULATED...

I *MEANT IT* WHEN I MADE HIM THAT PROMISE, BECAUSE HE SAVED ME FUCKIN' LIFE AN' I'LL NEVER FORGET IT. AN' WI' YOU, JAYSIS, I JUST GOT ARSEHOLED AN' MADE A DICK'VE MESELF. THERE WAS NOTHIN' MORE TO IT THAN THAT.

I LOVE HIM LIKE A BROTHER, TULIP.

I MEAN IT.

YOU'D FUCKING BETTER.

I WASN'T SURE IF I DID THE RIGHT THING, LEAVING YOU ALONE WITH HIM...

NO, YOU WERE GREAT.

I WANTED A CHANCE TO YELL AT THE IDIOT. LAST THING I NEEDED WAS JESSE OVERHEARING.

YOU THINK IT WORKED?

I HOPE SO. HE SEEMED GENUINELY HURT WHEN I SAID HE HAD ULTERIOR MOTIVES. HE CAN BE SO SINCERE, YOU KNOW?

BUT I SOMETIMES WONDER ABOUT CASSIDY...

I DUNNO.

SO WHERE NEXT?

JESSE SAID SOMETHING ABOUT GOING WEST. HE MENTIONED ARIZONA, UTAH, LIKE THAT.

WELL, YOU'VE GOT MY NUMBER.

YOU REMEMBER, GIRLFRIEND-- IF THE SHIT EVER HITS THE FAN, NO MATTER WHERE YOU ARE OR WHAT KIND OF TROUBLE YOU'RE IN, YOU CALL ME...

I'LL COME RUNNING.

YOU TAKE CARE.

YOU TOO. SEND ME A POSTCARD.

TULIP?

YEAH?

YOU THINK MAYBE YOU SHOULD TELL JESSE AFTER ALL?

OH JESUS, AMY...IT'S LIKE I TOLD YOU, IT'D BE A TOTAL MESS...

I KNOW.

LOOK, YOU TOLD ME HOW NEAT EVERYTHING WAS FOR A WHILE, YOU AND JESSE WITH YOUR BUDDY CASSIDY ALONG FOR THE RIDE. AND I DO KNOW WHAT THAT'S LIKE, BELIEVE ME.

IT'S JUST... I MEAN IN MY EXPERIENCE, IF EVERYONE'S COOL LIKE THAT AND THEN SOMETHING LIKE THIS HAPPENS...

THINGS CAN NEVER BE THE SAME AGAIN.

OLD FAMILIAR FACES

GARTH ENNIS - Writer   STEVE DILLON - Artist

MATT HOLLINGSWORTH - Colorist

CLEM ROBINS - Letterer   AXEL ALONSO - Editor

PREACHER created by GARTH ENNIS and STEVE DILLON

FRENCH ONION SOUP.

CHEESE-BURGER.

CHICKEN POT PIE.

PETE'S DINER

SO WHAT EXACTLY IS IT YEH THINK THE INDIANS CAN DO FER YEH? OH, YEH COULDN'T PASS US THE SUGAR, COULD YEH?

IT'S RIGHT THERE IN FRONT OF YOU.

AYE, BUT IF I PICK IT UP ME HAND'LL GO ON FIRE. NICE ONE.

IT'S SOMETHIN' THE ANGEL SAID TO ME...

SEEMS GENESIS IS KINDA WIRED INTO MY HEAD, MEMORIES AN' ALL. LOTS OF STUFF I NEED TO KNOW BUT CAN'T REMEMBER -- GOD, HEAVEN, EVEN SOMETHIN' ABOUT THE SAINT...

SO HOW CAN THE NAVAJO HELP WITH THAT?

MAYBE SOME MYSTIC DRUG BULL-SHIT OR OTHER. I DUNNO.

POINT IS TO FIND OUT EXACTLY WHERE THE LORD'S HIDIN' OUT. NO MORE STUMBLIN' AROUND HOPIN' WE'LL RUN ACROSS HIM AN' GETTIN' DISTRACTED: WE CAN GO STRAIGHT FOR THE SON OF A BITCH.

ISN'T THIS FUCKIN' MENTAL, WHEN YEH THINK ABOUT IT?

I MEAN HERE YEH ARE, YEH'VE GOT THE BODILESS OFFSPRING OF A DEMON AN' ANGEL STUCK IN YER HEAD, AN' YER TRYNNA REMEMBER *ITS* MEMORIES SO YEH CAN GO AN' CONFRONT GOD --DO YEH NEVER STOP AN' THINK, JAYSIS, THIS IS MAYBE A WEE BIT WEIRD?

YEAH, BUT ANYTIME I DO, I JUST THINK HOW THE GUY SITTIN' NEXT TO ME CAN BENCH A DAMN STATION WAGON. WE'RE WAY PAST THE WEIRDNESS THING, CASS.

HEH.

CAN I HAVE MY COFFEE BACK, PLEASE?

OR TO PUT IT ANOTHER WAY...

YOU KNOW, SEEING AS WE'RE TALKING ABOUT RECOVERING MEMORY AND THAT SORT OF THING, HAVE YOU THOUGHT ABOUT SEEING A SHRINK?

WHAT?

WELL...SHRINKS ARE FOR ASSHOLES...

COULDN'T AGREE MORE, MATE. ASSHOLES.

BUT WHY...?

MM--'CAUSE ALL THEY DO IS CHARGE A GODDAMN FORTUNE TO LISTEN TO FOLKS SPEW OUT CRAP THEY OUGHTTA BE ABLE TO FIGURE FOR THEMSELVES, OR ELSE CONVINCE 'EM THEIR GRANDADDY FUCKED 'EM IN THE ASS.

...AN' BEFORE YOU ASK, NO, GRAN'MA MADE SOUP OUTTA HIM BEFORE I WAS BORN.

AYE, AN' THAT REPRESSED MEMORY STUFF'S BOLLICKS, ANYWAY. IT'S JUST A DICK-HEAD LICENSE FOR RICH PEOPLE, YEH KNOW, "MY DA SMACKED ME, SO IT'S OKAY FOR ME TO ACT THE PRICK"...

RIGHT. SO WHO TURNED THE VOLUME OF IGNORANCE UP TO ELEVEN?

JAYSIS, WHO CARES? IT DOESN'T MATTER IF IT'S THE POWER'VE THE OCCULT OR JUST SOME SORT'VE HYPNOSIS--THE POINT IS IT *WORKS*.

OH FUCK AYE, I'VE SEEN IT MESELF.

HE PUTS YEH INTO A TRANCE AN' TAKES YEH OVER, AN' WHEN YEH COME OUT'VE IT YEH KNOW YER PROBLEM: LIKE YEH'VE A CURSE ON YEH, OR YEH SHOULDN'T'VE DONE *X, Y* AN' *Z* TEN YEARS AGO. THAT'S WHY YEH CAN'T GET A HARD-ON.

THAT'S JUST AN EXAMPLE, LIKE, BUT YEH KNOW WHAT I MEAN.

I DON'T KNOW ABOUT THIS...

REALLY?

I GOTTA ADMIT, NEW ORLEANS IS A HELL OF A LOT MORE APPEALIN' THAN GODDAMN ARIZONA. NEARER, TOO.

ARE YOU SERIOUS?

DIFFERENT METHOD, SAME RESULT.

IS HE ANYTHING LIKE YOUR OTHER *MATE*, THE ONE WHO TURNED OUT TO BE A SERIAL KILLER AND ALMOST MURDERED US ALL?

WELL, NOBODY'S *PERFECT*...

I'M TELLIN' YEH, TULIP, IT WORKS EVERY TIME. THIS MATE'VE MINE'S FANTASTIC...

NO.

...SUHRUNNKUHH UHHNUHH, UH TRUHHMUHV HUVMUH FUHBLUHFF HUBB-MUHA SUHH UHUH UHMUH WHUHH, UH UHRUHZUHVA BUHYA BUHH SUH MUH-MUMUHDUH CUVRAH HUBFUH!*

*SO IRONICALLY ENOUGH, THE TRAUMA OF HAVING MY FACE BLOWN OFF HELPED ME TO SEE THE ERROR OF MY WAYS, AND I RESOLVED TO BE THE BEST SON MY MOM AND DAD COULD EVER HAVE HOPED FOR!

UHFUHYUHNY, MUHLUV NUHLUHHAVAH THUH...*

IS THAT A FACT?

MM!

*UNFORTUNATELY, MOM LEFT NOT LONG AFTER THAT...

JUST CURIOUS, BUT IS THIS STORY OF YOURS ANYWHERE NEAR DONE?

JUH GUH SUHHH!*

*JUST GETTING STARTED!

SWELL.

THAT'LL BE EIGHT-FIFTY. DON'T LET THE DOOR HIT YOU IN THE ASS ON THE WAY OUT.

SHUH THUH!*

*SURE THING!

THIS *ALWAYS* HAPPENS...

NO IT DOESN'T. ANYWAY, WHY CAN'T WE PLAY MY TAPE?

'CAUSE IT DISTURBS ME, YOU LISTENIN' TO THAT STUFF. WHAT'S WRONG WITH THE KING? CAN'T GO WRONG WITH THE KING.

YES, YEH FUCKIN' CAN. LOOK, I'VE GOT THIS ONE HERE--

KLIK

LONDON IS FLOODING, IIIIII LIVE BY THE RIVAAAHH--

KLIK

AN' YOU LIGHT MY MORNIN' SKYYYY, BURNIN' LUHUVV...

KLIK

KNEW A CRACK DEALER BY THE NAME OF PETAH, HAD TO BUCK 'IM DOWN WIT' MY NINE MILLIMETAH...

I JUST DON'T SEE HOW YOU CAN BE SO SENTIMENTAL ABOUT THE SOUTH, WHEN YOUR CHILDHOOD WAS SUCH A TOTAL NIGHTMARE...

AYE, AN' WHAT ABOUT YER FIVE YEARS IN ANNVILLE? IF I'D HAD TO FACE THAT PACK'VE GOAT-RAPISTS EVERY SUNDAY, I'D'VE PUT A BLEEDIN' GUN IN ME MOUTH...

OH?

OKAY, YOU AIN'T. LIFE COULDA BEEN SWEETER.

LIQUOR STORE SOLD A LESS DRASTIC ALTERNATIVE. BESIDES, YOU'RE EXAGGERATIN', BOTHA YOU.

POINT IS, THE SOUTH IS GENERALLY WHERE I'M HAPPIEST. I BEEN TO CALIFORNIA, I BEEN TO THE EAST COAST, I BEEN ALL THROUGH THE DESERT --HELL, I EVEN WENT TO GODDAMN *FRANCE* ONCE, BUT THERE AIN'T ANYWHERE I FEEL MORE AT EASE THAN TEXAS.

SOMETIMES HOME IS JUST HOME, AN' THERE'S NO USE FIGHTIN' IT.

I DUNNO. I'VE SUCCESSFULLY FOUGHT MINE ALL ME LIFE.

WHAT'S SO GREAT ABOUT MARLBORO COUNTRY, THEN?

THE FOOD. THE HISTORY.

THE SKY.

THE SKY?

SURE. AIN'T A SKY IN THE WORLD LIKE WE GOT IN TEXAS. REAL DEEP BLUE TO THE HORIZON, AN' LITTLE WHITE COTTON BALLS DRIFTIN' ACROSS IT, TAKIN' THEIR OWN SWEET TIME. I USED TO LIE AN' WATCH 'EM ALL DAY.

MMM...

PLACE HAS A SENSE OF ITSELF, TOO. YOU CAN'T GO TEN YARDS WITHOUT TRIPPIN' OVER A SPOT SOME OL' BOY GOT SCALPED ON A COUPLE HUNDRED YEARS AGO, OR A RANGER TROOP MADE A STAND AN' GOT MASSACRED.

YOU EVER GO TO SAN ANTONE? HELL, THEY GOT THE ALAMO RIGHT THERE IN THE MIDDLE OF TOWN...

AN' LOOK AT THIS: BACON, EGGS AN' THAT'S THAT. HOW ABOUT SOME GRAVY, AN' SOME BISCUITS TO WIPE IT UP WITH?

...OR SO I'D IMAGINE...

YEH MEAN THAT GREY STUFF THEY MAKE OUT'VE BACON FAT? FOR JAYSIS' SAKE, JESSE, IT TASTES LIKE FUCKIN' SEMEN!

...BUT YOU KNOW WHAT I LIKE BEST ABOUT THE SOUTH?

MM?

IT'S THE WAY LIFE CAN GET REAL INTERESTIN', REAL FAST.

I THINK THAT MIGHT BE LESS TO DO WITH THE STATE OF TEXAS AND MORE WITH THE STATE OF JESSE CUSTER.

I SUPPOSE LIFE'S GONNA BE GETTIN' PRETTY FUCKIN' LIVELY FOR THE GOOD LORD ANY DAY NOW, WHA'?

UH-HUH.

I KNOW WHAT YEH WERE SAYIN' AN' EVERYTHING, BUT I STILL CAN'T GET ME HEAD ROUND IT. FINDIN' GOD, PUNISHIN' GOD--IT'S TOO BIG, TOO ABSTRACT.

ONLY IF YOU ALLOW IT TO BE.

HE DID WRONG. HE FUCKED PEOPLE UP. HE HAS TO BE MADE TO FACE IT.

YOU LOOK AT IT THAT WAY, HE'S JUST ANOTHER SON OF A BITCH.

BUT IT'S--IT'S *GOD*. IT'S THE CREATOR OF THE BLEEDIN' UNIVERSE...

ALL THE MORE REASON HE SHOULD DO RIGHT BY IT.

SEE THIS? THIS WAS JUST ABOUT PUT ON ME AT GUNPOINT. I NEVER REALLY, TRULY BELIEVED IN WHAT IT MEANT--BUT THAT AIN'T EVEN RELEVANT ANYMORE.

NONE OF IT IS: WHETHER YOU HAD FAITH AN' WERE CERTAIN HE WAS THERE, OR REFUSED TO BELIEVE HE COULD BE, OR JUST COULDN'T MAKE UP YOUR MIND, IT DOESN'T MATTER.

THE BIG QUESTION'S BEEN ANSWERED: HE'S THERE AN' HE CREATED US.

EXCEPT HE QUIT ON US WHETHER WE BELIEVED IN HIM OR NOT, AN' I FOR ONE CALL THAT A *GODDAMN BETRAYAL*.

WELL... HE'S MAYBE GOT DIFFERENT RULES THAN US...

THEN HOW COME HE STARTS RUNNIN' AS SOON AS IT LOOKS LIKE HE'LL BE CALLED TO ACCOUNT? DON'T TRY TELLIN' ME HE DON'T KNOW RIGHT FROM WRONG.

YEAH.

LIKE YOU SAY, BELIEF'S IRRELEVANT. HE EXISTS. SOMEONE *IS* RESPONSIBLE FOR ALL THE HORROR IN THE WORLD, BUT HE DOESN'T WANT TO ANSWER FOR IT.

AS WELL AS THAT, HE KILLED ME AND BROUGHT ME BACK TO LIFE JUST TO TRY AND SCARE JESSE. HE MADE MY DEATH A COMPLETELY MEANINGLESS VIOLATION.

I THINK HE'S A PIECE OF SHIT.

GOOD TIMES ROLLING

GARTH ENNIS - Writer   STEVE DILLON - Artist
PAMELA RAMBO and JAMES SINCLAIR - Colorists
CLEM ROBINS - Letterer   AXEL ALONSO - Editor

PREACHER created by GARTH ENNIS and STEVE DILLON

WHY?

HEY, WE'RE GONNA BE THERE BY TOMORROW NIGHT. IT AIN'T NO BIGGIE.

WE GIVE HIM A RIDE, WE PUT HIM ON A BUS, WE SAY GUHBUH, AN' WE GO ABOUT OUR DAY...

IT ISN'T FUNNY, JESSE!

I MEAN IT'S BAD ENOUGH HAVING McDRACULA WITH US, BUT *HIM* ?

AND SINCE WHEN WERE WE A CHARITY FOR WAIFS AND STRAYS, ANYWAY? ESPECIALLY ONES POINTING FUCKING HAND-CANNONS AT US?

OH, HE WASN'T GONNA HURT US, TULIP. YOU KNOW THAT.

LOOK, THAT GUY IS THE DUMBEST, MOST PATHETIC SON OF A BITCH ON THIS EARTH. HE IS A TESTAMENT TO GOD'S SENSA HUMOR. HE IS *ARSEFACE*...

BUT HE'S A SCARED, LONELY KID A LONG WAY FROM HOME, AN' I JUST AIN'T GOT IT IN ME TO TURN MY BACK ON THE POOR BASTARD.

I DON'T SEE WHY YEH DIDN'T JUST TELL HIM TO SHOOT HIMSELF...

HEY, YOU DIDN'T HAVE TO LOOK IN THEM BIG BROWN EYES.

I DON'T KNOW WHY YOU THINK IT'S SO FUNNY. YOU'RE THE ONE RIDING IN THE BACK.

SUITS ME!

FRENCH QUARTER, NEW ORLEANS:

PARKED.

CHECKED IN.

BEER.

GRUVUH!

WOULDN'T IT BE GROOVIER TO GO CHECK OUT THE BUS TIMES?

TUMURUH.

AND ANYWAY, AREN'T YOU UNDER-AGE?

SURE WHO THE FUCK'S GONNA CHECK HIS I.D.?

YOU CALL YOUR BUDDY?

AYE, HE'S MEETIN' US AT THE PLACE. AN' IS HE IN FOR A SHOCK...

GUESS SO.

NO, I MEANT AT ME KNOCKIN' AROUND WI' THE CLERGY.

THAT THAT THAT THAT'S HIM...

WHERE'S YOUR FUCKING PHONE?!

WHAT DO *YOU* WANT?

WHAT?

OH GOOD.

A *MINISTER?* AND-- LIKE A WHAT? SLOW DOWN, YOU'RE NOT MAKING ANY SENSE--

LOOK, NEVER MIND. I'LL SEND SOMEONE OVER.

NO, THE EIGHTEEN-YEAR-OLD MALT. YES, THAT ONE. AND ARE THOSE THE *BEST* CIGARS YOU'VE GOT?

AND ANOTHER MARTINI FOR THE LADY.

IT'S ME.

CALL DUKE, AND HAVE HIM MEET MILLY ACROSS THE STREET FROM THE RENO. TELL HIM CASSIDY IS THERE.

WHO?

BEFORE YOUR TIME.

TELL HIM NOT TO ATTEMPT ANYTHING DIRECTLY. THERE'S A WOMAN WITH THE PARTY. BRING HER.

DON'T TELL MAKO...

WHY ON EARTH WOULD I?

WHAT'S ALL THIS ABOUT, LILI?

IT'S ABOUT YOU AND I GETTING WHAT WE'VE ALWAYS WANTED, JONATHAN. IT'S ABOUT LES ENFANTS DU SANG FINALLY MADE REAL.

CALL ME WHEN IT'S DONE, WILL YOU?

I'LL BE HAVING A DRINK WITH A FRIEND.

SO I MEANT TO TELL YEH: XAVIER AN' ME, WE ... SORT'VE PARTED ON EVER SO SLIGHTLY BAD TERMS, LAST TIME ...

HOW BAD WE TALKIN' ABOUT? YOU WIN THE MILLENNIUM FALCON OFF HIM AT CARDS?

OR DID YOU TRY TO FUCK HIS GIRLFRIEND OR SOMETHING LIKE THAT?

KEEP THE CHANGE, HONEY.

JAYSIS, NO--

HELLO, CASSIDY.

AH! XAVIER! HOW'RE YEH?

GOOD SO FAR.

HAVE A SEAT--D'YEH WANNA DRINK? OH, WHO'S THIS? SORRY, THIS IS JESSE, TULIP AN' ARSEFACE.

I THINK I CAN WORK OUT WHICH IS WHICH. THIS IS JANIS.

HI, EVERY-ONE!

THIS IS CASSIDY, JANIS.

HELLO. HEY, HAVE WE MET BEFORE...?

AH...MAYBE, AYE. IT'S BEEN ABOUT FIVE YEARS SINCE I WAS LAST HERE.

OH, I ONLY CAME HERE IN THE FALL. BUT I'M SURE I'VE SEEN YOUR FACE BEFORE, SOMEWHERE...

SO DO YEZ WANNA DRINK?

WE CAN'T STAY LONG. ABOUT THIS THING I MIGHT BE ABLE TO HELP WITH...?

YEAH.

THIS MUST BE A FIRST. A MINISTER OF THE LORD TURNING TO VOODOO FOR ANSWERS.

I GUESS THE LORD JUST AIN'T WHAT HE USED TO BE.

I MEAN I'M SURE YOU'VE GOT ALL SORTS OF REALLY COOL PROPS AND STUFF, BUT IT SOUNDS TO ME LIKE YOU WOULDN'T BE DOING MUCH MORE THAN HYPNO-THERAPY...

I AGREE.

THAT IS WHAT IT SOUNDS LIKE. IT HAS THE SAME RESULT, WHICH I'M SURE YOU'LL AGREE IS THE OBJECT OF THE EXERCISE.

BUT TO ANSWER YOUR QUESTION ...WELL.

THERE WAS A VERY, VERY OLD LADY WHO LIVED A COUPLE OF BLOCKS FROM WHERE I GREW UP. PEOPLE WOULD GO TO HER FOR CURES AND THINGS--LAYING A TRICK, OR GETTING ONE TAKEN OFF, STUFF LIKE THAT...

SOMETIMES IT WORKED, OR SOMETIMES COINCIDENCE WAS ON HER SIDE, DEPENDING ON YOUR POINT OF VIEW. BUT PEOPLE BELIEVED IN IT ENOUGH TO KEEP GOING BACK.

I ONCE PLUCKED UP THE COURAGE TO ASK HER IF *SHE* BELIEVED IN IT. ALL SHE DID WAS SMILE --THIS SORT OF KNOWING, ENIGMATIC SMILE, YOU KNOW? SO: DO I ACTUALLY BELIEVE, TULIP?

SHE GET YOU STARTED?

PRETTY MUCH. I SUPPOSE I'M NATURALLY CURIOUS ABOUT THE WAY THE WORLD'S PUT TOGETHER, ANYWAY.

I STUDIED BIOCHEMISTRY AND PHYSICS FOR SEVEN YEARS. HEARD WHAT SOME OF THE TOP MINDS HAVE TO SAY.

AND NOT ONE OF THEM GAVE ME ANSWERS THAT WERE ANY MORE CONVINCING THAN THE ONES THAT OLD LADY DID.

141

TOMORROW NIGHT WORKS FOR ME. CASSIDY HAS MY NUMBER.

GOOD MEETING YOU BOTH, BY THE WAY.

YOU TOO, XAVIER.

...AND IF YOU GET A CHANCE, YOU OUGHT TO TRY THE GUMBO HERE. IT IS TO *DIE* FOR...

SO LOOK, THANKS FOR HELPIN' US OUT WI' THIS, YEH KNOW?

BUSINESS IS BUSINESS. BESIDES, I LIKE YOUR FRIENDS.

AYE. uh... ABOUT LAST TIME...

THAT'S NOT A CONVERSATION I WANT TO HAVE RIGHT NOW.

YUH?

GOOD GUY.

YEAH, I LIKED HIM. STILL CAN'T BELIEVE YOU'RE GOING THROUGH WITH THIS CRAP.

YEAH, OKAY, AGENT SCULLY. 'NOTHER DRINK?

NO, I THINK I'M GOING TO TURN IN.

HELL, REALLY?

YOU GUYS LOOK READY TO MAKE A NIGHT OF IT. I'M OKAY, I'VE GOT MY BOOK.

BESIDES, I AM *NOT* GOING TO SIT HERE AND WATCH HIM EAT GUMBO.

MENU

142

...WUH, UHDUHNUH BUHD SUDDLN DUH. UHD HUWA BUH GUH WUHH RUH QUADUH.*

*WELL, I DON'T KNOW ABOUT SETTLING DOWN. IT'D HAVE TO BE A GIRL WITH THE RIGHT QUALITIES.

AN' WHAT WOULD THEY BE, AS FAR AS YOU'RE CONCERNED?

WUH NUH...*

*WELL NOW...

FUH MUH, GUH LUGZUHNUH PUDUYUH. UH WUH WUHM UH CUH TUHG TUH, YUH NUH? SUHMUN UH CUH PUH MUH HUHDDUHDUH. SUHMUN HULUHWUHZ BUH THUH.

A SUHLMUH...*

*FOR ME, GOOD LOOKS ARE ONLY PART OF IT. I WANT A WOMAN I CAN TALK TO, YOU KNOW? SOMEONE I CAN POUR MY HEART OUT TO. SOMEONE WHO'LL ALWAYS BE THERE.

A SOUL MATE...

AYE. I JUST LIKE A FUCKIN' MASSIVE BIG PAIR'VE TITS, MESELF.

WHAT DO YOU GO FOR, JESSE?

PRETTY FACES.

AN' I SWEAR, THE TROUBLE I BEEN IN OVER PRETTY FACES...

YEH KNOW YER MAN HERE'S A VIRGIN, DON'T YEH?

NO SHIT?

FUCK!!

WAAAH!

RIGHT NOW IT'S SELF-DEFENSE, COCKSUCKER. WOMAN ALONE IN HER ROOM, THREE PILES OF SHIT WITH A KNIFE. NO ONE TO SAY DIFFERENT.

YOU LITTLE FUCKER, I BET IT NEVER ENDED LIKE THIS BEFORE--

NO!

I SWEAR TO FUCKING GOD WE WEREN'T GONNA HURT YOU! DUKE WAS BEING AN ASSHOLE! JESUS CHRIST, **PLEASE**!

SO WHAT WERE YOU HERE FOR?

I CAN'T POSSIBLY TELL Y--

I HEARD SHOOTING--

THEY'RE BACK THERE! TWO MEN! SOMEBODY KILLED THEM! *OH GOD IT'S HORRIBLE,* CALL THE POLICE!

ROOM Nos 31–35

OH JESUS, I CAN'T STAND BLOOD!

GUTS! BRAINS! IT'S HORRIBLE, I'VE GOT TO GET OUT!

..."I CAN'T STAND BLOOD." WHAT A *DICK.*

JESUS FUCKING CHRIST, LADY, WHAT IS IT WITH YOU?

SHUT UP, PISS-PANTS.

I WANT TO TALK TO THESE FRIENDS OF YOURS. SEE HOW THEY LIKE IT WHEN THEIR KIDNAPPEE GETS IN THEIR FACE WITH A HALF-DOZEN HOLLOW POINTS. BASTARDS.

BECAUSE THAT GUY IS REALLY STARTING TO MAKE ME WONDER.

AND ON THE WAY, YOU CAN TELL ME HOW *CASSIDY* FITS INTO ALL THIS...

147

NOW WHATEVER YEH DO, YEH MUSTN'T TAKE THE BAG OFF...

YEAH.

I'M SERIOUS, NOW. IT'S FOR YOUR OWN PROTECTION. *DON'T TAKE IT OFF.*

YEAH, YEAH. LET'S GO.

ROOM'S YOURS FOR A HALF-HOUR.

YOU MIND IF WE WAIT FOR OUR BUDDY?

PLEASE YOURSELF. DON'T STEP IN THE CUM.

TELL HIM WE'LL BE OUT FRONT.

148

SO WHAT DO YOU ASSHOLES WANT WITH CASSIDY?

UH, JONATHAN, SHE--

QUIET, MILLY.

WE WANT HIS POWER.

PERSONALLY, I WANT TO RIP HIS MOTHER-FUCKING HEAD OFF...

SHUT UP, MAKO.

WE WANT HIM TO DRINK FROM US, AND BLESS US WITH IMMORTALITY, THAT LES ENFANTS DU SANG WILL LAST FOREVER.

WHAT IS THIS LES ENFANTS SHIT?

LOOK, REALLY, SHE'S GOT--

MILLY.

WE ARE CHILDREN OF BLOOD, AND OF SHADOW, AND OF NIGHT. WE DRINK FROM VEINS AND ARTERY. OURS IS A PALE AND LANGUID PARADISE, AND IN OUR DREAMS WE WALK AS WOLVES AND FLY AS BATS.

AND PREY AT WILL UPON THE HUMAN HERD.

SOUNDS LIKE ONE BIG CIRCLE-JERK TO ME.

ARE YOU CASSIDY'S SOW?

WHUHNNGHH

THERE'S A TIME AND A PLACE, LILI...

GOT THE MESSAGE?

ABSOLUTELY NOBODY FUCKS WITH ME, DOGSHIT. THAT'S THE GOLDEN RULE.

YOU BUNCH OF PATHETIC FUCKING LESTAT WANNABES SHOULD JUST STAY DOWN HERE AND PRACTICE YOUR MASTURBATION. FORGET ABOUT CASSIDY. AND YOU: BITCH. YOU OPEN YOUR MOUTH TO ME AGAIN AND I'LL PUT A FUCKING BULLET IN IT.

HMMM. FOLLOW HER, MAKO.

EH?

BILL HICKS. VIRUS WITH SHOES, THAT'S HIS LINE, AIN'T IT?

I DIDN'T KNOW *YOU* WERE INTO BILL HICKS...!

GODDAMN RIGHT.

FUCKIN' JAYSIS! RELENTLESS, GOAT BOY, ROCKERS AGAINST DRUGS SUCK--YEH LIKE ALL THAT STUFF?

UH-HUH.

MATTER OF FACT, I EVEN SAW HIS SHOW ONCE.

WHAT?

WHAT?!

MET HIM, TOO.

LEMME SEE NOW... FEW YEARS BACK I'M IN DALLAS OR AUSTIN, I DON'T RECALL WHICH, AN' I WANDER INTO SOME CLUB OR OTHER FOR A DRINK...

"DIDN'T EVEN KNOW WHAT KINDA PLACE IT WAS 'TIL I GOT INSIDE. JUST HAPPENED TO BE THE NEAREST TO WHERE I CRASHED THE TRUCK."

"SEE, THIS WAS BACK IN THE ANNVILLE DAYS, WHEN I WAS MOSTLY SO DRUNK I COULDN'T SEE THROUGH A LADDER WITH TWO TRIES..."

A HALF-HOUR WEEKLY SHOW THAT I WILL HOST, ENTITLED "LET'S HUNT AND KILL BILLY-RAY CYRUS..."

IT'S A FAIRLY SELF-EXPLANATORY PLOT, *uh,* EACH WEEK WE LET THE HOUNDS OF HELL LOOSE AND WE CHASE THAT JARHEAD, NO-TALENT CRACKER ASS-HOLE ALL OVER THE GLOBE 'TIL I FINALLY CATCH THAT FRUITY LITTLE PONYTAIL OF HIS IN THE BACK, PULL HIM TO HIS KNEES, PUT A SHOTGUN IN HIS MOUTH LIKE A BIG BLACK COCK OF DEATH--

BKOOOMM!

AN' WE'LL BE BACK IN NINETY-FIVE WITH "LET'S HUNT AND KILL MICHAEL BOLTON"...

THANK YOU VERY MUCH. I'M JUST TRYING TO RID THE WORLD OF ALL THESE *FEVERED EGOS,* THAT ARE TAINTING OUR COLLECTIVE UNCONSCIOUS--AND MAKING US PAY A HIGHER PSYCHIC PRICE THAN WE IMAGINE.

IN FACT, THAT'S HOW I PITCHED IT TO THE NETWORKS, EXACTLY--

CAN I GET A BLACK COFFEE?

YEH LUCKY FUCKIN' BASTARD. WASN'T HE BRILLIANT, BUT?

HE WAS THE GREATEST GODDAMN COMEDIAN I EVER SAW.

"WE'RE PRO-LIFE" ...ALL THE LITTLE KIDS: "PLEASE DON'T ADOPT ME! PLEASE DON'T ADOPT ME!"

"WE'RE YOUR NEW CHRISTIAN PRO-LIFE PARENTS"..."PLEASE, GIVE ME THE SATAN-WORSHIPPING FAMILY DOWN THE BLOCK. THE ONES THAT HAVE THE GOOD ALBUMS."

"BEFORE THAT NIGHT, I NEVER EVEN HEARD OF THE GUY. ONLY TOOK ABOUT TEN MINUTES FOR ME TO SEE I WAS NEVER GONNA FORGET HIM."

"ARE YOU PROUD TO BE AN AMERICAN?"

I WAS LIKE--I DUNNO, I DIDN'T HAVE A LOT TO DO WITH IT...MY PARENTS FUCKED THERE, THAT'S ABOUT ALL...

...WHEN YOU WIN? YOU GO INTO THIS SMOKY ROOM WITH THE TWELVE INDUSTRIALIST CAPITALIST SCUMFUCKS WHO GOT YOU IN THERE ...AN' A BIG GUY AN' A CIGAR: "PUFF-PUFF ROLL THE FILM PUFF-PUFF-PUFF"...

AN' IT'S A SHOT OF THE KENNEDY ASSASSINATION FROM AN ANGLE YOU'VE NEVER SEEN BEFORE THAT LOOKS SUSPICIOUSLY OF THE GRASSY KNOLL...AN' THE LIGHTS GO UP AN' THEY GO TO THE NEW PRESIDENT: "PUFF-PUFF-PUFF ANY QUESTIONS?"

"UH, JUST WHAT MY AGENDA IS!"

AFTER THE SHOW I HAD A BIG SLOPPY GRIN ON MY FACE FOR ABOUT A HALF-HOUR. JUST FELT ...I DUNNO, LIKE I WAS GRATEFUL I'D SEEN THIS GUY, THAT HE WAS THERE SAYIN' THESE THINGS ...

NEXT THING I KNOW HE'S AT THE BAR BESIDE ME.

I GUESS THAT MAKES TWO OF US.

AN' A COUPLE MONTHS AFTER THAT, HE WAS DEAD.

THANKS-- HOLY SHIT, YOU'RE A PREACHER!

PANCREATIC CANCER. HE KNEW, TOO. GUY KEPT GOIN', KEPT PERFORMIN', WITH THE LICENSE GRANTED A DYIN' MAN TO SAY WHAT HE LIKES WITHOUT FEAR.

NOW I DIDN'T AGREE WITH EVERYTHING HE SAID OR BELIEVED, BUT BY GOD I COULD SEE THAT GUY STOOD UP AN' TOLD THE TRUTH AS HE SAW IT: NO COMPROMISE, NO RETREAT.

"ANNVILLE BEIN' THE CULTURAL DINGLEBERRY IT WAS, I DIDN'T GET TO HEAR HE DIED FOR SOME TIME.

"ONCE I DID--WELL, I DECIDED I WAS ABOUT THROUGH COMPROMISIN', TOO."

THE LONG TRAIL
BAR

"SO I STOOD UP AN' TOLD THE TRUTH AS I SAW IT, AN' WAS RIGHTLY REWARDED FOR MY TROUBLE."

THERE'S A LESSON IN HERE, SOME-WHERE...

NOT THE ONE YOU'RE THINKIN' OF.

NO, FOLKS DON'T LIKE THE TRUTH. THAT'S THE POINT.

IT'S EASIER LYIN'. STOPS US HAVIN' TO FACE UP TO TROUBLE WHEN IT COMES ALONG. TO DO WRONG INSTEADA RIGHT.

I SHOULD KNOW, 'CAUSE I LIED TO MYSELF FOR FIVE GODDAMN YEARS OF EATIN' SHIT AN' PRAISIN' JESUS...

BUT I HATE A LIE, CASS. MY OWN MOST OF ALL. THEY KEEP US CRAWLIN' IN THE DUST WHEN WE COULD AN' SHOULD BE CLIMBIN' FOR THE STARS.

BILL HICKS KNEW THAT, DIDN'T HE?

AN' A GUY WHO'LL TELL THE TRUTH IN THIS BULLSHIT WORLD, HE'S WORTH HIS WEIGHT IN GOLD.

PSSST!

HEY...!

C'MERE!

BUT--

WHY AIN'T YOU IN THE ROOM-- WHUP--

C'MERE!

THE ROOM'S A LITTLE BIT HOT RIGHT NOW. I HAD TO SHOOT SOME PEOPLE IN IT.

WHAT?

COPS ARE ALL OVER THE HOTEL. IT HAS TO DO WITH CASSIDY, WHO WE NEED TO HAVE VERY STRONG WORDS WITH RIGHT AWAY.

BUT-- BUT ARE YOU OKAY?

YEAH, FINE. I CHECKED OUT THE BAD GUYS' PLACE AND SHOT THEM UP A LITTLE BIT, YOU KNOW. THERE WERE QUITE A LOT OF THEM, AND ONE GUY NEARLY GOT ME WITH A THROWING KNIFE--

BUT I KNOW YOU'LL BE COOL WITH THAT, BECAUSE YOU KNOW YOU CAN TRUST ME TO HANDLE MYSELF.

LET'S GO.

166

ARE YOU SURE YOU'RE OKAY? YOU OUGHT TO BE IN SHOCK, AT LEAST.

I'M NOT A VERY SHOCKABLE PERSON, LILI.

WHAT DOES CONCERN ME IS THE GENERAL LEVEL OF SQUEAMISHNESS AMONG *LES ENFANTS.* YOU NEVER SAW *NOSFERATU* HAVING TO GO HOME BECAUSE "I JUST ABOUT SHIT MY PANTS"...

THEY'LL BE BACK TONIGHT. THEY KNOW THERE'S TOO MUCH AT STAKE.

ACTUALLY, THIS KIND OF REMINDS ME OF *ROGER...*

I'D RATHER NOT THINK ABOUT ROGER AT THE MOMENT. I MIGHT ACCIDENTALLY REMEMBER ONE OF HIS POEMS.

YES, BUT THE JOKE'S ON HIM, ISN'T IT?

HE TURNED HIS BACK ON US WITH HIS FIRST ROYALTY CHECK AND WENT OFF TO REINVENT GENRES OR SOMETHING--AND HERE *WE* ARE ON THE VERGE OF ETERNAL LIFE...

IN FACT, THE FIRST THING I'LL DO IS PAY THE LITTLE PRICK A VISIT--

HELLO? MAKO?

IT'S HIM.

IT'S CASSIDY. I FUCKING GOT THE BASTARD.

167

BITCH LED ME TO SOME MINISTER GUY --THEY'RE BOTH WITH HIM NOW. FUCKER HASN'T CHANGED A BIT.

OH, I'LL STAY ON HIM ALL RIGHT. I AM *GLUED* TO THE MOTHER-FUCKER.

...I SWEAR TO YEZ, I THOUGHT THEY'D ALL'VE WISED UP AN' GROWN OUT'VE IT! LES ENFANTS DU WANKY FUCKIN' SANG, JAYSIS, THE *LAST* THING I EXPECTED WAS FOR THEM TO STILL BE ON THE GO!

SO WHAT, YOU JUST FORGET TO MENTION THAT THESE PEOPLE ARE AFTER YOU? EVEN THOUGH YOU KNOW WE'RE GOING TO NEW ORLEANS?

TULIP COULDA BEEN HURT, YOU KNOW.

...THAT IS, IF SHE WASN'T ONE HUNDRED PERCENT SELF-RELIANT AN' ABLE TO HANDLE ANYONE DUMB ENOUGH TO MESS WITH HER, I MEAN.

FACT REMAINS, CASS: YOU FUCKED UP.

I KNOW, JAYSIS, I'M SORRY! BUT I NEVER EVEN THOUGHT, YEH KNOW?

JESSE, HONESTLY, YEH SHOULD SEE THE FUCKIN' STATE'VE THESE EEJITS. THERE'S *TWO DOZEN'VE* THEM, AN' I'LL BET YEH A MILLION DOLLARS RIGHT NOW YEH COULD FLATTEN THE LOT'VE THEM SINGLE-HANDED -- WITHOUT USIN' YER WORD EVEN *ONCE.*

WE'LL PROBABLY NEVER HEAR FROM THEM AGAIN, AN' I REALLY *AM* SORRY.

ALL RIGHT?

HEY, DEE!

I'VE BEEN WAITING FOR YOU, JANIS. I REALLY NEED TO KNOW ABOUT THAT THING...

UH, NOT RIGHT NOW, DEE. XAVIER'S HERE.

WELL- GREAT, ISN'T HE THE ONE WE SHOULD ASK?

UM...NOT REALLY...

YOU SEE, I SORT OF DIDN'T TELL HIM I WAS GIVING YOU THE SPELL OUT OF HIS BOOK...

WHAT?

HE TAKES THIS STUFF VERY SERIOUSLY, YOU KNOW? HE'S ALWAYS TELLING ME YOU SHOULDN'T MESS WITH IT..

BUT WHAT IF YOU GOT IT WRONG? I COULD'VE BEEN WASTING MY TIME TRYING TO *GET* THAT SON OF A BITCH!

SHH, XAVIER'S GONNA HEAR YOU!

LADIES

I MEAN WE'RE MEETING PEOPLE OVER THERE, WE'RE SUPPOSED BE GOING OUT TO THE BAYOU TONIGHT...

DEE?

LADIES

OKAY?

FINE.

JUST OFF TO POINT PERCY AT THE PORCELAIN, AS THEY PROBABLY DON'T SAY DOWN UNDER...

ANYWAY, AT THAT MOMENT THE SNAKE WILL BE UPON YOU, AND--COMBINED WITH THE EFFECTS OF THE TRANCE--WILL BE ABLE TO OPEN YOUR MIND TO ARPE-REPOSOIR.

THE SNAKE WILL BE UPON ME...THAT'S A REAL SNAKE YOU'RE TALKIN' ABOUT, RIGHT?

I THOUGHT YOU WEREN'T AFRAID OF THEM?

SIT YER-SELF DOWN, LOVE. YER BOYFRIEND'S JUST SCARIN' THE SHITE OUT'VE US WI' THE AMAZIN' POWER'VE VOODOO.

I AIN'T. I JUST DON'T WANNA BE THE WORLD'S BRAVEST SNAKEBITE VICTIM, IS ALL.

MY ROUND, INDIANA.

IT ISN'T ACTUALLY THAT KIND OF SNAKE.

NO?

AH, ONE DIXIE, TWO DIET COKES, ONE J.D. AND ICE AND A KRAKATOA HURL WITH EXTRA CHERRIES.

AN' A HEROIN ON THE ROCKS FOR ME.

AND HOW DO YOU FIGURE THAT, EXACTLY?

BUT YEH HAVEN'T, BECAUSE YEH CAN'T DENY HOW YEH FEEL ABOUT ME.

I KNOW IT AN' YOU KNOW IT, TULIP: YOU WANT ME AS MUCH AS I WANT YOU.

OKAY, LET ME TELL YOU WHAT YOU'RE DOING HERE: YOU'RE WRITING A STORY. YOU'VE GOT THE PLOT AND THE DIALOGUE FROM MELROSE PLACE AND FUCKING BAY-WATCH, AND YOU'RE WRITING YOURSELF A LITTLE STORY IN YOUR HEAD...

THE TROUBLE IS YOU'RE USING ME AS ONE OF THE CHARACTERS.

YEH'D'VE TOLD HIM.

I DIDN'T SAY ANY-THING TO JESSE BECAUSE I DIDN'T WANT HIM FINDING OUT HIS BEST FRIEND WAS AN ASSHOLE TRYING TO STICK ONE IN HIS BACK. BUT YOU KNOW WHAT?

THAT'S EXACTLY WHY I SHOULD HAVE TOLD HIM.

YOU STAY THE FUCK AWAY FROM ME IN THE FUTURE, CASSIDY.

BOLLICKS.

I MIGHT HAVE SEEN THE SAME ONE.

HAD THE OTHER GUY, NOT SEAN CONNERY. WASN'T TOO BAD, THOUGH. FELLA FROM *ALIEN* PLAYED THE VILLAIN, AN' YOU HAD THIS REAL BADASS VOODOO MOTHER-FUCKER FELL INTO A CASE OF SNAKES...

AND JANE SEYMOUR.

OH YEAH.

ANYWAY, THE VOODOO GUY, HE HAD THIS WHOLE OUTFIT-- BONES, TOP HAT, SKELETON PAINTED ON HIS CHEST, LITTLE SNAKES EVERY-WHERE...GUESS I WAS EXPECTIN' YOU TO DO SOME'VE THAT SHIT, YOU KNOW?

REALLY?

MAYBE

I WILL,

JESSE.

SNAKES IN THE GRASS

GARTH ENNIS - Writer   STEVE DILLON - Artist

PAMELA RAMBO - Colorist

CLEM ROBINS - Letterer   AXEL ALONSO - Editor

PREACHER created by GARTH ENNIS and STEVE DILLON

...AND OH I MEAN I'M NOT SURPRISED I'VE ENDED UP WITH A GUY LIKE XAVIER BECAUSE I'VE ALWAYS BEEN ATTRACTED TO SPIRITUAL MEN, YOU KNOW? LIKE A GUY WHO CAN REALLY SEE THROUGH TO THE INNER ME?

OF COURSE I MEAN IT'S NOT LIKE WE DIDN'T HAVE TO WORK AT IT, 'CAUSE I'M VIRGO AND HE'S CAPRICORN AND EVERYTHING AND MERCURY WAS LIKE SO IN THE ASCENDANT THE NIGHT WE MET--

SO YOU-- YOU BELIEVE IN THE STUFF HE DOES TOO, YEAH?

OH FOR SURE! FOR SURE, YEAH! I MEAN YOU ONLY HAVE TO LOOK AT HIM TO KNOW HE'S A HUNDRED PERCENT REAL ABOUT IT!

AND I MEAN IT'S LIKE I SAY, HE'S A SPIRITUAL GUY, HE FEELS STUFF... I MEAN I KNOW HE REALLY WANTS TO USE THIS GIFT HE'S GOT TO HELP PEOPLE, YOU KNOW?

I MEAN THIS FRIEND OF MINE, DEE?

SHE HAD LIKE THIS BOYFRIEND, THIS REALLY BAD GUY WHO WAS JUST TOTALLY ABUSIVE TO HER? AND I MEAN I GOT HER THIS SPELL OF XAVIER'S SHE CAN DO TO FUCK THE GUY UP? LIKE GUARANTEED MISFORTUNE?

AND THIS IS HELPING PEOPLE?

... IT HELPS DEE.

I MEAN YOUR FRIEND CASSIDY, IT'S SO WEIRD BECAUSE HE LOOKS SO FAMILIAR TO ME, YOU KNOW? BUT I *CAN'T* HAVE SEEN HIM BEFORE BECAUSE I WASN'T IN TOWN WHEN HE WAS LAST HERE...

BUT XAVIER KNOWS HIM.

YEAH BUT IT'S KIND OF STRANGE, YOU KNOW? 'CAUSE I THINK THEY USED TO BE REALLY CLOSE AND THEN SOMETHING HAPPENED, LIKE I THINK CASSIDY DID SOMETHING?

OH?

YEAH, REALLY, I MEAN XAVIER WON'T REALLY TALK ABOUT IT, BUT LIKE WHEN CASSIDY CALLED HIM UP ABOUT HELPING YOU GUYS OUT, I THOUGHT MAYBE HE WASN'T GOING TO?

BUT HE LOOKED KIND OF SAD AND HE SMILED A LITTLE BIT AND HE SAID--"FOR OLD TIMES' SAKE."

BUT CASSIDY, YEAH, I WISH I COULD REMEMBER WHERE I'VE SEEN HIM...

ARPE-REPOSOIR. YOU ARE ON HIM. UPON HIM. AROUND HIM. *IN* HIM.

SLIDE INTO HIS SPIRIT. UNCOIL THE SECRETS TANGLED THERE.

AND SPEAK TO ME.

VOODOO FEATURES PRESENTS

A MIND'S EYE PRODUCTION

OF A JESSE CUSTER FILM

WAIT. WHERE IS HE?

IN A PLACE HE FEELS AT EASE.

GO ON.

GOD ALMIGHTY

THE SAINT OF KILLERS

THOSE DAMN ANGELS

AND THE DUKE

IN

SO JONATHAN, WE WERE KIND OF TALKING, AND WE THINK THIS IS ALL MAYBE GETTING A LITTLE INTENSE...

OH?

DON'T GET ME WRONG, BEING IN LES ENFANTS DU SANG IS WAY COOL AND EVERYTHING, BUT...WELL, YOU KNOW, DRESSING UP AND DRINKING EACH OTHER'S BLOOD IS ONE THING, BUT THAT CHICK LAST NIGHT HAD A GUN...

I'M OFFERING YOU A CHANCE AT THE REAL THING HERE, DO YOU UNDERSTAND? I'M TALKING ABOUT ETERNAL LIFE. I'M TALKING ABOUT UNBELIEVABLE POWER.

BUT SHE SHOT MILLY UP THE ASS, MAN...

YES, I KNOW SHE SHOT MILLY UP THE ASS...LILI, WOULD YOU SHOW THEM WHY THAT'S NOT GOING TO HAPPEN AGAIN?

DRESSING UP AND DRINKING BLOOD? IS THAT THE ABSOLUTE LIMIT OF YOUR VISION?

FUCKING COOL...!

DON'T PLAY WITH THEM. ANYONE DISCHARGING A ROUND AND BLOWING OUR COVER IS GOING TO GET THE NEXT ONE IN HIS FACE.

THE THING I DON'T UNDERSTAND IS THIS *MINISTER*... I MEAN WHY WOULD AN UNDEAD GUY HANG WITH SOMEONE LIKE THAT?

DOES IT MATTER? WHAT'S HE GOING TO DO, BEAT US TO DEATH WITH HIS BIBLE?

WELL, FUCK IT. SO LONG AS I GET MY SHOT AT CASSIDY.

WHAT IS IT WITH YOU AND HIM ANYWAY, MAKO?

A LITTLE MATTER OF SOMEONE ONCE HAVING GOT THE SHIT KICKED OUT OF HIM...

I WASN'T READY.

WHATEVER. ANY SCORES TO BE SETTLED, WAIT 'TIL *AFTER* HE'S GIVEN US WHAT WE WANT.

NOW, THESE PEOPLE ARE AN UNKNOWN QUANTITY. THE WOMAN IN PARTICULAR IS *VERY GOOD*, WHICH IS WHY THE REST OF LES ENFANTS ARE GOING IN FIRST. UZIS OR NOT, THEY'RE NO USE AS ANYTHING BUT CANNON FODDER.

BUT THEY WILL ALLOW US A CLEAR RUN AT CASSIDY...

YES, BUT HE'S TOTALLY UNKILLABLE -- AND EVEN IF HE WASN'T, WE NEED HIM ALIVE TO DO WHAT WE SAY...

HOW EXACTLY ARE YOU GOING TO TAKE HIM, JONATHAN?

YOU LEAVE THAT TO ME.

YET A QUESTION REMAINS. A FOUL AND TERRIBLE DOUBT THAT FESTERS TO THIS DAY.

"WAS THERE A *WILL* BEHIND IT ALL, BEHIND THIS CHAIN OF TRAGEDY AND HORROR?"

BUT WHO?

WHO WOULD CAUSE THE DEATHS OF SO MANY?

WHO WOULD GIVE A MAN THE MEANS TO DAMN HIMSELF, WHEN FOR TEN LONG YEARS HE'D TRIED SO HARD TO CHANGE?

WHO WOULD THROW THE DEVIL'S LIFE AWAY, AS IF IT WERE AN AFTERTHOUGHT?

WHO WOULD SEEK TO REPLACE A TIRED AND SOULSICK ANGEL OF DEATH, GROWN WEARY OF HIS BURDEN?

WHO WOULD LET LOOSE A FORCE OF SUCH UNPRECEDENTED IRE AND FURY TO ENACT THE WRATH OF HEAVEN? WHO WOULD HAVE THE LAWS OF PARADISE ENFORCED BY THE THUNDER OF HIS GUNS?

WHO WOULD *WANT A SAINT OF KILLERS?*

AND WHO COULD ARRANGE THE PLAYERS...CROSS THEIR PATHS...AND THEN SIT BACK AND LET MEN'S NATURE TAKE ITS COURSE?

TWENTY MILES TO THE EAST A BAND OF SCUM APPEARED FROM OUT THE GATHERING BLIZZARD, HOPELESSLY LOST.

A DOZEN WORTHLESS SONS OF BITCHES: AND WHO-EVER SENT THE STORM THAT TURNED THEM FROM THEIR COURSE, SURELY THE HAND THAT CAUSED SUCH WOEFUL MISDIRECTION WAS NOT GOD'S?

WHERE'S JANIS AWAY?

HER CAR. SHE BROUGHT A THERMOS OF COFFEE.

BUT THAT DOESN'T GIVE YOU A LICENSE TO START ACTING LIKE A JERK AGAIN, OKAY?

TULIP, I'M NOT JUST GONNA GO AWAY, YEH KNOW. I'M NOT GIVIN' UP WHEN I KNOW YEH'RE LYIN' TO YERSELF LIKE THIS...

CAN I ASK YOU A QUESTION?

SURE--

WHY ARE YOU BEING SUCH A DICK?

HOW AM I A DICK?

YOU KEEP HITTING ON ME BEHIND JESSE'S BACK WHEN I'M NOT INTERESTED IN YOU. HOW'S THAT FOR STARTERS?

AYE, LIKE FUCK...!

NO, REALLY. I'M NOT INTERESTED.

I *KNOW* THE GOOD LORD IS A EVIL PIECE OF SHIT. I SEEN THE THINGS HE CAUSED, AN' THE THINGS HE LET HAPPEN. AN' I KNOW HE'S RUNNIN' SCARED OF ME AN' THIS *GENESIS* I GOT INSIDE ME, 'CAUSE OF WHAT HE'S GOT COMIN' WHEN I CATCH UP TO HIM--

SO HOW, GODDAMMIT? HOW DO I FIND THAT *SKULKING SON OF A BITCH?*

THIS IS WHAT IT SAW WHEN THEY HAD IT HOGTIED, PILGRIM. *WATCH REAL CAREFUL.*

HEY, THAT'S THE ASSHOLE I SEEN BEFORE...!

BUT HOW CAN IT WANT TO ESCAPE, IF IT'S BARELY EVEN SENTIENT?

BECAUSE ITS POWER IS DIRECTIONLESS. IT'S AN INFANT; IT SEEKS A STRONGER CONSCIOUS- NESS TO TELL IT WHAT TO *DO...*

THE THING IS, ANY MENTAL CONTROL EXERTED OVER IT WILL DRASTICALLY REDUCE ITS STRENGTH. PHYSICALLY CAPTIVE AS IT IS NOW, IT'S APPALLINGLY POWERFUL--BUT IT HAS NO INHERENT MEANS OF CHANNELING THAT POWER.

WERE IT EVER TO GET LOOSE, THE CARNAGE INFLICTED BEFORE IT FOUND A HOST TO CONTROL IT... I DREAD TO THINK, DeBLANC.

YOU DREADED RIGHT, BOY.

HOW STRONG IS IT?

IT'S...GOD, YOU CAN'T MEASURE SOMETHING LIKE THIS. IT'S OFF THE SCALES. WITHOUT A DOMINANT WILL TO EXERT SOME MEASURE OF RESTRAINT, IT COULD DO *ANYTHING*...

YOU COULDN'T STOP IT, RUN FROM IT, OR HIDE FROM IT: NOT EVEN IF YOU WERE GOD ALMIGHTY.

WHO, I CAN'T HELP BUT NOTICE, *LEFT US* THE MINUTE IT ARRIVED...

SO I GUESS YA KNOW WHAT YA GOTTA *DO*, HUH?

...YEAH.

I HAVE TO LET GENESIS TAKE CONTROL.

AW, DEADLY. JUST THE STUFF FOR FRIGGIN' ABOUT IN CEMETERIES AT TWO IN THE MORNIN', WHA'?

DON'T START YOUR VOODOO RITUAL WITHOUT IT.

HEH.

...

JAYSIS--!

DEE--OH JESUS-- XAVIER --

XAVIER!!

DEE?

HELP!

PRICE OF NIGHT

GARTH ENNIS - Writer   STEVE DILLON - Artist

PAMELA RAMBO - Colorist

CLEM ROBINS - Letterer   AXEL ALONSO - Editor

PREACHER created by GARTH ENNIS and STEVE DILLON

KILL HER-- KILL HER--

WHAT THE FUCK IS GOIN' ON?!

YOU KNOW WHAT I'M GONNA DO WITH THAT PIGSTICKER, YOU DON'T QUIT WAVIN' IT AT ME?

SHIT!

UHM GUH BUH UH STUHH!

A STAR?

YOU?

YUH! MUZDUN SUJJUH HUHZ GUHNUH SUHN MUH!

GENE SERGEANT, REVEREND CUSTER. YOUNG ARSEFACE HAS TOLD ME ALL ABOUT YOU.

AH AM INDEED GONNA SIGN THE BOY, TO MAH OWN PUHSONAL RECORD LABEL. HIS IMPROMPTU PUHFORMANCE IN BOURBON STREET LAST WEEKEND CONVINCED ME HE HAS THE POTENTIAL TO GO A LONG, LONG WAY...

YOU THINK?

INDUBITABLY, SUH. YOU SEE BEFORE YOU A READY-MADE ICON FOR AMERICAN YOUTH.

YUH UHKUH?

YEAH--

YEAH, DEADLY.

LET'S YOU AN' ME HAVE A WEE CHAT, WHA'?

WE SHOULD TALK, TULIP.

XAVIER?

WE TRIED TO FIND YOU, YOU KNOW, FOR--

THE FUNERAL WAS YESTERDAY. IT WAS A PRIVATE AFFAIR.

XAVIER... I AM SO SORRY...

IT WASN'T YOUR FAULT. WE BOTH KNOW EXACTLY WHERE THE BLAME FOR THIS LIES.

YOU KNOW SOMETHING ABOUT HIM, DON'T YOU? SOMETHING BAD?

BAD.

YOU KNOW... I HATE CASSIDY, TULIP. I'M LEFT WITH NO CHOICE BUT TO LOATHE HIM FOR WHAT HE'S CAUSED. BUT REALLY, IN MY HEART OF HEARTS, AND EVEN AFTER EVERYTHING THAT'S HAPPENED... I HONESTLY DON'T BELIEVE THAT HE'S AN EVIL MAN.

JUST CARELESS. AND THOUGHTLESS.

AND TERRIBLY, TERRIBLY WEAK.

WHAT HAPPENED BETWEEN THE TWO OF YOU, ANYWAY?

A WOMAN.

CASSIDY SEDUCED HER WHILE I WAS OUT OF TOWN.

SEDUCED...THEY WERE DRUNK AND THEY FUCKED. IT WAS HER AS MUCH AS HIM.

THE POINT IS, WE WERE SO CLOSE I TRUSTED HIM IMPLICITLY. I NEVER IMAGINED HE WOULD DO A THING LIKE THAT, THAT THE THREAT OF IT COULD COME FROM HIS DIRECTION.

HE'S BRILLIANT AT BEING YOUR BEST FRIEND TULIP. MEN RESPOND TO THAT ROGUEISH FREE SPIRIT OF HIS ON SOME BASIC MALE LEVEL: A COMRADE, A GOOD MATE, AS HE HIMSELF WOULD SAY. I DON'T THINK IT'S CALCULATED, I THINK HE'S REALLY LIKE THAT...

BUT THAT'S WHY I'M HAVING THIS CONVERSATION WITH YOU, AND NOT WITH JESSE.

EVERY TIME HE CAME TO TOWN WAS AN OCCASION. I LOVED HIM SO MUCH I LET HIM CLIMB RIGHT INSIDE OF ME, UNTIL I COULDN'T IMAGINE LIFE WITHOUT HIM.

AND THEN HE LET ME DOWN.

YOU THINK THAT'S HOW IT ALWAYS IS WITH HIM?

I THINK HE GOES THROUGH LIFE WITHOUT A SENSE OF CONSEQUENCE.

HE DIDN'T CARE THAT LES ENFANTS MIGHT BE DANGEROUS, THAT THEY'D STILL BE OUT TO GET HIM AFTER WHATEVER HAPPENED BEFORE. IT DIDN'T EVEN OCCUR TO HIM.

TOO BAD FOR JANIS, MM?

IT'S JUST CASSIDY, TULIP.

SHIT HAPPENS IN HIS WAKE.

217

WHAT'S WRONG WITH YOUR VOICE?

GOT ME HEAD CHOPPED OFF ON MONDAY NIGHT. THIS IS JUST 'TIL EVERYTHING GROWS BACK TOGETHER.

I WASN'T SURE YEH'D STILL BE HERE...

IF I'D KNOWN YOU WERE COMING BACK, I'D'VE MOVED.

I'D'VE RUN FOR MY LIFE.

DEE... WHAT'S GOIN' ON, WOULD YEH TELL ME?

IT'S A VOODOO THING. YOU FIRE AN EMPTY GUN AT THE PERSON'S PICTURE, THE ONE YOU WANT TO HURT, YOU CURSE THEM.

IT'S SUPPOSED TO REALLY FUCK THEM UP.

MY FRIEND JANIS TOLD ME ABOUT IT. HER BOYFRIEND DOES ALL THAT STUFF.

OH, SHITE.

YEH DON'T REALLY BELIEVE ALL THIS BOLLICKS, DO YEH?

I USED TO GO OUT WITH A GUY WHO DRANK BLOOD AND DISINTEGRATED IN SUN- LIGHT. YOU LEARN TO KEEP AN OPEN MIND.

HOW'S MY BABY?

HE'S FEELIN' OLD.

OLD AN' TIRED AN' GUILTY.

HEY, IT WASN'T YOUR FAULT...!

OH, BUT THAT POOR GIRL...I BARELY EVEN KNEW HER, BUT SHE GOT TOO CLOSE TO THIS CRAZY ROAD I'M ON AN' IT JUST REACHED OUT AN' KILLED HER.

WE GOTTA GET ON AN' FINISH THIS THING, TULIP, 'FORE ANY MORE INNOCENT BLOOD GETS SPILT.

YEAH. ABOUT... CASSIDY...

YEAH, YOU KNOW HE AIN'T COMIN' WITH US?

WHAT?

HE'S STAYIN'. CONVINCED ARSEFACE TO TELL SERGEANT HE'S HIS UNCLE.

HOW?

DON'T KNOW. THE BOY AIN'T GOT SENSE ENOUGH TO SPIT DOWNWIND, I GUESS THAT HELPED.

CASS IS HOPIN' FOR A SHARE 'VE ANY MONEY THEY MAKE -- WHICH I FIGURE'S GONNA BE ABOUT A NICKEL, BUT I'M SORTA GLAD CASS'LL BE THERE TO LOOK OUT FOR HIM. I AIN'T TOO SURE ABOUT MISTER GENE SERGEANT.

SORRY, WHAT WERE YOU SAYIN'?

...OH, NOTHING.

WHERE TO?

GONNA TAKE THE ANGEL'S ADVICE, TRY AN' ACCESS GENESIS DIRECTLY. I THINK I KNOW EXACTLY WHAT I NEED FROM IT.

GO WEST, YOUNG TULIP.

YOU UPSET ABOUT CASSIDY?

MM?

HE PROMISED YOU HE'D STAY 'TIL IT WAS FINISHED, AS I REMEMBER. SO MUCH FOR HIS WORD.

HE JUST GOT DECAPITATED, HONEY. THAT'LL PLUMB RATTLE SOME FELLAS.

FAME AN' FORTUNE BE FUCKED! HAVE YEZ ROOM FOR A BASTARD?